Winter of Summers

Winter of Summers

Michael Faudet

Andrews McMeel
PUBLISHING®

For Lang,

Love looks pretty on you.

Winter of Summers

Introduction

Winter of Summers began in the early hours, while I was sitting outside my hotel suite in Dubai, waiting for the Arabian dawn to break.

I hadn't planned to write anything that morning but the words just started to flow, as if like magic, and there was no stopping them.

They became my constant companion, following me wherever I went.

Be it relaxing on a sandy beach on an island in Fiji, or strolling up the steps of the Sydney Opera House at dusk, I just couldn't escape them.

And then one morning, as the mist rolled in from the sea, the words bid me farewell.

The very last piece written at the kitchen table of my home in New Zealand. Sipping a strong black coffee laced with whiskey.

I really hope you enjoy my fourth book, and find within its pages a particular poem or piece of prose that becomes special to you.

And whenever you read *Winter of Summers*, may my words become your traveling companion.

Wherever life takes you.

All my love,

—Michael x

ARABIAN DAWN

She possessed a rare beauty that was slowly revealed with every word she spoke—like how an Arabian dawn softly breaks the darkness with the gentlest of hands.

Into Depths

Into depths of ocean blue—
    your summer eyes
    reflect in mine,
    your smile,
    a rousing,
    rising sun—
    greets a morning
    made for two.

We swim,
    my love—
    beneath a sea
    billowing white,
    upon a bed
    of coral pink,
    against the muted
    light of dawn,
    sun-kissed bodies
    gently sink.

YOU ARE BEAUTIFUL

The one thing we all have in common is our differences. Embrace your uniqueness. You are beautiful just the way you are.

TURNED ON

Oh, when it comes to being turned on, she said, it's simple.
You have to first unbutton my mind before unclipping my bra.

WE SIPPED

We sipped our sadness
in glasses poured—
from a bottle filled
with emptiness.

A LIGHTHOUSE IN A STORM

It was a love that defied the change of seasons, the ebb and flow of tides, the transition from day to night—a lighthouse in a storm.

TRIGGER WARNING

There is no trigger warning,
    when the gunman
    pulls the trigger,
    no safe space,
    when a bullet takes a life,
    no sanity,
    when insanity is elected,
    and no humanity,
    when the rifle
    is protected—
    but not the child.

RUN

When you know you're in a toxic relationship don't just walk away. Run.

A WORLD OF PRETEND

The sweet taste of sugar
quickly soured,
but I smiled
through the bitterness
at the end of our end—
for when a heart
so badly broken
refuses to mend,
all that remains
is a world
of pretend.

A PERFECT WORLD

I often found myself drifting away from reality. Seeking sanctuary within a world of impossible daydreams. Where our love refused to die.

WHEN YOU LEFT

I still remember the gentle squeeze of your hand before you said goodbye. Like a little patch of sunshine found on a cold winter's day.

ISOLATION

If only we could escape the prying eyes and virtuous finger-wagging of this small-town circus.

To run away and hide our love in some distant foreign city. Where the past ceases to exist and freedom is found in the company of strangers.

Until then, let's just close the shutters, bolt the door, and switch off the lights.

And kiss in the dark shadows of glorious isolation.

CLOSER

Whenever you are away from me, the closer we become.

A TIRED BUTTERFLY

Our love—
    a tired butterfly
    trapped in a glass jar,
    wings beating
    like two hearts
    refusing to let go,
    oblivious—
    to the reality
    of fate,
    disguised
    as hope.

I'VE TRIED TO FORGET YOU

I've tried to forget you, to move on, to run away—only to be held hostage by the relentless thought of "what could have been?"

PLEASE STAY

Please stay,
    just a little longer,
    let not the ticking
    of a clock
    force our arms apart,
    for time loses meaning,
    becomes nothing—
    without you.

COLLABORATION

Love is a story created by you but written by another's pen.

Sharjah

My love for you—
　　comes from a place
　　where stars sing
　　to strangers,
　　and desert sands
　　hold the sea
　　in a delicate
　　embrace,
　　under a crescent moon
　　your kisses sweet—
　　lips sprinkled
　　with sugar dust,
　　pale pink,
　　rosewater infused
　　rahat lokum.

Where magic
　　wakes with the dawn,
　　the morning call
　　to prayer—
　　if scent made a sound
　　it would be this,
　　the rarest
　　of perfumes.

It is here
　　from a city of books,
　　my love for you
　　is written.

IN YOUR ARMS

In your arms
  my anxiety sleeps,
  where dreams
  of calm seas begin,
  the tranquility
  of knowing
  I am loved—
  my salvation.

When the Dark Clouds Came

You were always the optimist. The girl who could find the tiny patch of blue in a stormy sky. You once said, *"Love can find a way to overcome any obstacle."* I tried my best to believe you but my eyes could never see past the rain and howling wind. If only I could have shared your enthusiasm and shaken off the self-doubt that gripped my heart. Maybe things might have turned out differently. Perhaps you would have stayed.

I never found the courage to tell you just how broken I was. How I had nothing more to give. My glass empty, while yours remained half full.

I'm sorry I hurt you like I did.

For everything I said.

When the dark clouds came.

BOOKS

My preferred way to travel is not a plane but a book. How wonderful it is to be transported somewhere new without having to leave your bed.

LITTLE DID I KNOW

Little did I know
how much you
meant to me—
my regret,
the bitter aftertaste
of hindsight,
walking alone
without the hand
that held my life
together.

A SINGLE KISS

Just when I thought I understood love, all that it could possibly be, you came along and explained its true meaning with a single kiss.

THE REAL YOU

I never lost sight of the real you—the goodness that lived within your heart. Even when you did your best to convince me otherwise.

HOW IT FEELS

How it feels—
    when cool water
    meets parched lips
    on a hot summer's day.

How that first mouthful
    of coffee ice cream tastes,
    when we're stoned
    watching *Black Mirror.*

Falling rain—
    captured by dappled light
    as it hits the leafy green.

The breathtaking beauty
    of a storm rolling in
    across the bay.

When a cat crawls
    under the covers
    and curls up against
    naked skin.

A sip of strong coffee
    in the morning.

How that slow kiss
    under the stars
    felt last night.

How words,
    no matter how many,
    can never express
    this wonderful feeling—
    the happiness
    I feel with you.

JUST WHEN

Just when we think we know someone, the stranger returns
to remind us just how wrong we are.

SUMMER

It was like you held a tiny glowing sun in the palm of your hand. Your delicate fingers—rays of golden light. Each gentle touch—a warm breeze caressing my skin.

Reminding me of every summer I had ever known.

CHANGE

When change comes it is often gradual.

A city skyline rising up toward the clouds as the centuries pass.

How trees in a park welcome the seasons with calendar leaves.

The first strand of gray hair discovered in the mirror.

And then there are the exceptions to the rule. Those moments when change happens in an instant. Catching you completely unaware—a bolt from the blue.

Like when you're at the beach. Standing knee deep in the water. Eyes staring back at the shore and a rogue wave suddenly hits you from behind. Knocking you off your feet. Throwing you under the swirling water.

Everything you knew, the stability you took for granted—all swept away in a blink of an eye.

"I'm leaving you."

At first I struggled to come to terms with those three devastating words.

My heart breaking in an instant. The shock wave resonating throughout my heaving chest—the tears streaming down my cheeks.

Followed by the body-numbing emptiness.

My nights spent hiding away from the world with *our song* playing on repeat on an iPod. My mind slowly tearing itself apart. Searching for a reason. Trying to find an explanation that made some sense of it all. Lost in a maze with no exit in sight.

As the weeks passed, the crippling pain began to fade and the inevitable *acceptance* finally arrived in a neatly wrapped, emotional package. Containing a sprinkling of anger and a generous spoonful of steely resolve.

It was like my eyes were finally open and I could see the relationship for what it was. A daily climb up a steep staircase carrying a piano. You holding one side with your fingertips, barking orders, while I was left to do all the heavy lifting.

"Well, fuck you!"

When change comes it is often for the best.

A forest rising up from the cinders of a bushfire.

How the sun greets the sky after a storm.

The first step taken when you're ready to move on.

THE SILENCE

On a good day
    I could hear a pin drop,
    the distant humming
    of a bumblebee,
    a soapy bubble
    popping in a bath.

But somehow,
    I didn't hear
    the deafening roar
    of my heart breaking.

Just the silence
    when you were gone.

SWEET NOTHINGS

It's not that I don't enjoy our little conversations. I love them.
It's just that sometimes I wish you would say nothing and just
fuck me.

JUST ONE MORE DAY

Just one more day,
        you said to me,
        as your dawn
        was gently breaking,
        I replied,
        with a heavy sigh,
        it is an eternity
        to be waiting.

If only time
        could be divided,
        the passing hours
        thrown away,
        if only I could
        send you a sunset,
        the dying seconds
        of a day.

WHEN I FIRST SAW YOU

When I first saw you, it was like a star had fallen to the Earth and landed in a field of white roses lit by a full moon.

BLISS

I love how you become aroused. How the words slip from your lips just that little bit quicker. How the pupils in those calm blue eyes dilate when I pull down your panties.

Your eyes closing as you feel the warmth of my breath, the soft touch of my mouth, pressed up against your swollen clitoris.

Liquid honey running down my chin.

Firm hands pushing your willing thighs apart. The intensity of the pleasure making you grind your wet pussy against my face.

The wave building, breaking without warning, sweeping you away in the moment.

The orgasm exploding.

Once.

Twice.

Your body forced upright, fists clenched, as the third hits you hard between your twitching legs.

My head rising up, resting on the side of your flushed neck—lips kissing you.

Our arms holding each other tight.

Not letting go.

The rhythm of two hearts beating as one.

Bliss.

ALONE AGAIN

There are those
   who walk,
   the lucky ones run,
   and then there's us—
   the unfortunate few,
   who stumble
   at the first hurdle,
   always left behind
   in this wretched race—
   others call love.

FIVE SECONDS

I wanted you so badly. If happiness could be broken down into units of time, it would be those magical five seconds when you said you felt the same way about me.

BURNT LETTERS

Perhaps it's the vodka talking, but as I hold your latest letter in my hands, I feel compelled to tell you about the conflicting emotions that have been raging through my heart. It is not something I want to do, but I cannot think of any other way of finding some sense of resolution. To quote that tired cliché, I truly find myself between a rock and a hard place.

Before I continue, please bear with me, my love, while I pour another glass and summon the last drop of courage before it drains from me completely. I never thought it would take this much strength to push a pen between the blue lines of a blank piece of paper.

I wish I could explain exactly how your words touch me. How they make my whole body ache for you. (Tonight is no exception.) And the more I read what you wrote to me, the stronger the desire to hold you in my arms becomes. *My impossible dream.*

What was once an explosion of raw sexual tension played out in sentences, has now become an unbearable state of insatiable frustration. I can see the rosy red apple hanging on the tree but it is always just out of reach. *If only I could stop reading your letters.*

But I can't.

So with a match lit, I have decided to do what I should have done months ago. To burn every one of them.

It's time to accept that we can never be. To put an end to this beautiful torture we so willingly inflict on each other. I hope you understand why I have to walk away now.

Like the ocean that stands between us, the reality of the different lives we live is a gap too wide for either of us to cross.

Please, I beg you, do not reply to this letter.

Let me take comfort in the glowing embers of our past.

Leave me alone with the memories of what never was.

My hands cupped, warmed by the dying flames of a love reduced to cinders.

ALCHEMY

You kissed me—and that's when everything in my world changed forever. The alchemy of instant connection. Like when two Lego bricks click together.

IGNORANCE

Ignorance is cultivated by those who prefer to plant the seeds of doubt rather than have the courage to speak the inconvenient truth.

SUNSHINE GIRL

You were the lover—
    the sunshine girl
    who took me
    by the hand,
    and showed me
    where my heart
    was hidden,
    deep down
    beneath a pool
    of rainy tears,
    your glowing smile—
    breaking through
    the heavy clouds,
    chasing away
    the last strands
    of wispy sadness,
    your warm kisses—
    painting my sky
    a brilliant blue.

The First Time We Met

We loved to spend our summer nights outside.

Hands holding icy cold Pepsi bottles, lips sucking on paper straws, sitting on a flat rock, legs dangling over the edge, toes skimming the still water of the lake.

Your old portable radio tuned to an '80s station. Duran Duran singing "Rio." The chorus carried away by a warm breeze blowing through the swaying trees.

Our conversation tracing back to the first time we met.

—

"I often wonder if it was destiny, or maybe a perfect alignment of the stars, or something even more magical that brought us together," you said, kissing my hand.

"I believe it was just sheer luck. Being in the right place, at the right time. Of course, how we fell in love was quite a different matter. It was fate. For how could anything this wonderful, this magnificent, be of this earth?"

WE HELD NOTHING BACK

We shared everything. It was just the way it was between us. We held nothing back. Even the last tiny square of chocolate was always carefully broken in half.

My Sunday Muse

There was something rather pleasantly serene about the state of post-orgasm.

The blushing glow of happiness and contentment upon our cheeks, hair messy, legs still trembling with pleasure—laying on a bed that felt like a soft cloud floating across a calm summer sky.

My fingers tracing the delicate curve of your breast, while your smiling eyes wandered, your mind drifting away to a place where thoughts gathered.

"I love you."

There was no immediate response from Sophia.

"Oh, sorry, I was away with the fairies," she replied suddenly. "I love you too."

"Looks like you were deep in thought."

Sophia grinned. "Well, I was thinking about how our perspective of the world is corrupted. How the images and narrative so often presented in the media, and especially social media, is frequently flawed and, in many cases, skillfully manipulated to promote somebody else's agenda."

I laughed. "I love it how your head can just jump from wild sex to pop culture in a matter of moans."

Sophia poked me hard in the ribs and burst out laughing too. "What do you think about that? How we have moved away from reality and fallen into this abyss of unreality."

"Well, to be honest, I think we've given up on seeking *the truth*. It's become a task few people are willing to undertake these days. It's been relegated to the too-hard basket. It seems like searching for actual facts and taking the time to cross-check them is sadly a dying art."

"I agree," Sophia replied, reaching under the sheets to find her crumpled panties. "Perhaps an even greater travesty is our intellectual laziness."

"Interesting. I'm all ears," I said.

Sophia slid her feet into her panties and pulled them up in one smooth action without pausing from the conversation. "Rather than do the research and find the evidence that supports a point of view, too many people instead choose the far easier option. To run with the first thought that pops into their heads and then waste all their mental energy to convince themselves, and others, *they are right*. Worse still, is the dreadful habit of parking their brains in some dead-end street and simply parroting the opinions of the mob. Selling out their integrity for some mindless clicked *likes* and dumb-ass smiley faces."

"Perhaps the world is slowly going insane and doesn't realize it."

"No, I disagree," Sophia said, brushing a lock of hair from her face. "I believe we've reached a point in history where we know exactly the stupid path we are sleepwalking along but simply don't care enough to wake up and change direction."

"Lemmings jumping off the cliff," I muttered, picking up the notepad and pen that sat on the bedside table.

"Exactly! Hey, what are you doing?"

"You just inspired me to write something."

—

Social Mediocrity

Dumb it down,
rip it up,
burn free speech
to the ground.

Don't dare offend,
just pretend,
be a sheep
inside the bubble,
content to bleat,
on repeat—
the silly nonsense
idiots say.

Ignore the facts,
do not retract,
hold on tight
to your flawed opinions.

Never disagree,
just appease,
sell your intellect
to the lowest bidder.

The Language of Flowers

You spoke the language of flowers. Every scented word an explosion of color. Falling from your rosy lips—how unfurled petals kiss the morning dew.

RESTLESS

When a dream comes true, it never ceases to amaze me how quickly the restlessness returns. Like when you're enjoying a delicious chocolate mousse and begin to wonder whether you should have ordered the profiteroles.

THE BREAK UP

"Have you told him?" Lucy asked, her arms wrapped around Anna's slender waist.

Anna laughed, "Yes, I told him. He got the message loud and clear."

Lucy kissed Anna hard on the lips and stared into her coffee-colored eyes. "I'm so proud of you. Tell me, what did you say to Heath? I'm dying to know."

Anna slid her hand under Lucy's yellow tee and kissed her neck. "Well, I didn't exactly speak to him in person, but I left him a note. It certainly did the job. He moved out on Wednesday and I haven't heard from him since."

"So, what did you write?" Lucy asked, barely containing her excitement.

"Well, it went a little like this."

—

Spare me the sweet nothings, the endless talk of campfires and forest wandering. Shove those marshmallows up your ass. Pack up your woolly hat, the hiking boots, and the rest of your well-curated disguise. You patronizing fake!

Hiding behind your "oh so perfect" hipster designer beard, faux namaste greetings, and smug, shit-eating grin.

Rip up those little notes of platitudes, the cringe-worthy poems, and the fading Polaroids you stuck up on my fridge.

And while you're at it, take your wanky collection of whiny, folksy, rubbish records with you.

Leave nothing behind.

Not a single trace that you ever existed.

Including that fucking boring book of origami you gave me for my birthday.

I know who you really are, Heath.

I've seen the little angry man lurking inside of you.

The nasty, possessive, jealous troll, who lashes out after necking too many of your bullshit bottles of craft beer. The bully who hits first and then sobs later. You pathetic excuse for a human being.

Just get the fuck out of my life.

You mansplaining piece of trash!

A SUMMER STORY

A summer story—
 the sea sings blue,
 below indigo sky
 of darker hue,
 rolling waves break
 over splashing legs,
 the cry of seagulls
 flying overhead,
 a Frisbee thrown
 to leaping dog,
 sandcastles crushed
 under stomping foot,
 scurrying crabs
 on seaweed rocks,
 while sailing boats sleep
 in moonlit docks,
 our whiskey sipped
 with salty lips,
 around driftwood fires
 dance swaying hips,
 beneath shooting stars
 warm kisses tell,
 a tale of lovers
 slowly bewitched—
 by summer's
 hypnotic spell.

WHO AM I?

We live so many lives in a single lifetime that it is often difficult to reconcile the person we once were with the stranger staring back at us in the mirror.

The Final Chapter

The dark circles
    under these eyes
    tell my story,
    cigarette burns
    on pale skin
    my words,
    like a broken book—
    its pages
    ripped out,
    only the ending
    left to be written.

Sleeping Beauty

Véronique.

So beautiful. So familiar. How smoothly it rolls off my tongue whenever I say it.

Véronique. Véronique. Véronique . . .

I cannot begin to count the number of times I have said your name over the years. Tracing the letters across your naked back, in that moment of calm—after fucking each other senseless beneath the sheets.

Véronique.

Do you remember the first time I spoke your name?

—

The Hysteria Club was packed. Standing room only. A sea of dancing bodies in front of me. Music thumping, spotlights spinning— flickering images of Andy Warhol projected onto screens.

I weaved through the crowd, pausing every so often to look for a new route, a slim gap, any opportunity to squeeze past and get to the front of the stage.

Then it happened.

The girl standing next to me collapsed to the floor.

—

All you needed was a little air.

That's what you told me.

So I took you outside and we stood on the corner, two strangers leaning against an old brick wall by the club. Saturday night traffic, horns honking, cruising bumper to bumper along the boulevard.

That was the very first time you told me your name.

My ears straining to hear it over the traffic noise. I had to ask you again. When I repeated it back to you, I struggled to pronounce it correctly.

You burst out laughing.

I tried to hide my embarrassment. My eyes staring down awkwardly at my feet as you said your name again.

"Véronique," I said, sounding out each syllable with careful precision.

"Perfect!" you replied with a beaming smile. Your pale blue eyes staring deeply into mine.

And that's when everything changed in a split second.

I was struck by a sudden thunderbolt of overwhelming emotions.

Giddiness.

Goosebumps.

An intoxicating cocktail of excitement, attraction, and desire.

You reached out for my hand and held it in yours. "Now I've told you my name, I'm dying to hear yours."

Just as I was about to say it, you leaned in and kissed me quickly on the lips. Silencing me in an instant.

"No rush," you said with a coy smile. "Come, walk with me a little."

"Sure," I said. "We could head down to Chinatown if you want. Perhaps get some dumplings. I know a late-night place that makes incredible ones."

"How did you know? I fucking love dumplings!"

"Serendipity, I guess," I replied laughing.

You squeezed my hand and pulled me closer.

Your lips gently touching my ear.

"I just love it when the stars collide," you whispered.

———

Véronique.

How many times have I said your name tonight?

And all the other nights.

Sitting here by your hospital bed waiting for you to wake up.

Holding your hand. Brushing your hair. Recounting all the stories we wrote together.

Can you hear me, my love?

I haven't slept much lately. And when I do, the nightmares return.

Jagged images flashing out of sequence.

Your naked body crumpled on the bathroom floor. The shower running. Flashing ambulance lights.

Cradling you in my arms. Heavy raindrops exploding in slow motion on the pavement. *She just needs a little air . . .*

The doctors said there was nothing I could have done. The brain tumor on the X-ray confirmed it. But I can't stop myself from thinking, *if only I had gotten home five minutes earlier.*

All I can do now is hope for a miracle.

Pray those beautiful eyes will open again.

And our stars will collide once more.

You

I always thought you meant the world to me. I was wrong. You mean much more than that. Even the universe doesn't come close.

LOVE ON MUTE

We watched the rain fall
  outside my window,
  wintery gray static—
  playing silently
  on a glass television,
  your head resting
  on my shoulder,
  passing a joint
  between lips,
  that said nothing
  and everything,
  in the same breath.

DENIAL

Do not be fooled by my air of nonchalance, the hesitation in my words, for deep down it is all just a hopeless deception. It is my unbridled fear of rejection that keeps me trapped in this sorry state of denial. Can you see the cracks appearing in this wall I have built? Like a dam dangerously close to bursting—my love a raging torrent waiting to break free.

EMPTY WORDS

There are plenty
of other fish in the sea,
you said sitting by
the ocean,
never knowing
what it's like
to live your life
in a shrinking pond—
fast becoming
an empty puddle.

HATERS

Don't listen to their bullshit—
just jealousy in disguise,
the bitter brooding envy
of shallow, spiteful lives.

And when they swing
the wrecking ball,
watch it swing
and miss its mark,
only to swing
back again,
and hit them
twice as hard.

COFFEE WITH THE EX

You said I was a lost cause. A hopeless case. Somebody who wouldn't amount to anything. Yet here I am, proudly standing tall. Content in my own skin and happy with my life.

And here you are, sipping an expresso. Telling me you always knew I would be successful. Trying to crawl back into my world again. A shocked expression plastered on your twisted face as I close the door behind me.

ACE OF HEARTS

And with a sudden
    swish of curtains drawn,
    the magic went away.

Your love for me
    a vanishing act,
    performed with
    sleight of hand.

The Ace of Hearts—
    the card I held,
    the one you
    gave to me,
    you took it back,
    no longer whole—
    but torn apart
    in two.

SWEET CORRUPTION

How wonderful it is to wander in this valley of sweet corruption. Where fingers walk between the banks of a flowing river, and lips taste the nectar of summer peaches, left to ripen in the sun.

CONSEQUENCES

What was I thinking? The truth was, I wasn't. My head in the clouds, ego pulsing through my veins, my cock doing all the decision-making. Convincing myself it would be just a one-off. A quick thrill. The seemingly fitting conclusion to weeks of flirty exchanges, that secret kiss in the hallway when you were leaving, the exchange of texts late at night while my wife was sleeping.

I have no excuses for what happened next. The lunchtime motel hook-ups when I was supposed to be at work, eating a sandwich at my desk. The lies spun from guilty lips that hid my shame beneath a beaming smile. The hurried showers taken when I walked in through the door at night, before sitting down to a wonderful dinner as if nothing had happened.

And when the damning receipt was found in the pocket of my trousers, the proof of infidelity, the evidence that exposed me for the cheating asshole I was, what did I do? I lied again. Only this time, I had nowhere to hide, nowhere to run, I was just another fucking cheater. A low-life piece of shit, standing in a laundry wringing my hands and waiting for my marching orders.

But it wasn't me who left was it?

The rotten twist of fate that lives with me still. The recurring nightmare that continues to haunt me.

Leaving the office late at night. The elevator doors opening in the basement. Casually walking into the underground parking lot and finding Jenny dead. Slumped inside her Mustang. Engine running. A blue hose attached to the exhaust pipe, the other end pushed into a partially open window, the slim gap stuffed with dirty towels.

You said you loved me. You told me you would leave her.

That's all the note said. Pinned to the windshield by a window wiper.

I didn't have the courage to go to the funeral. Instead I called in sick that day. It wasn't long after, I quit my job too. The endless speculation by my co-workers as to why Jenny took her own life was too much for me to bear.

She seemed so happy.

The words they kept repeating, gathered around the water cooler, while I acted just as surprised and shocked. Doing my best to conceal the paralyzing fear that somehow the truth of our affair would eventually be revealed.

Only my wife knew the real story. Refusing to accept the reality of my despicable conduct. Stoically standing by her wretched man. Her forgiveness given with a hug, causing me to break free from her arms and run to the bathroom. Vomiting into the toilet. The acrid aftertaste of betrayal on my breath. Face flushed, staring into the mirror, knowing I would never forgive myself.

—

There are consequences to every action we take. Some for the better, others for the worse. And always one that we regret for the rest of our lives.

JUST FOR NOW

I surrendered
    to the constant,
    that was the cradle
    of your arms,
    rocking me to sleep—
    like the ebb and flow
    of a restless tide,
    that never tired
    or stopped to think,
    how kisses flowed
    from silent lips,
    beneath sighing trees
    our love complete,
    no questions posed
    in happiness found—
    how rare it is to find
    the impossible,
    if just for now
    and only once.

ALL ABOUT YOU

I love how you take control, your eyes staring into mine. My hard cock throbbing beneath the grip of your tight fingers. Long legs straddling my waist. Your fierce smile giving way to a loud moan as you grind your wet pussy against my waist. Fucking me not for love, or even my pleasure. This is all about you and I wouldn't want it any other way.

BLUE SKIES

We are like hot-air balloons. To fly—we first have to cut loose the deadweight that is holding us back.

IN LETTERS SENT

The things I wrote
in letters sent,
to fall in love
the words intent,
each sentence came
and sadly went,
my soaring heart
now in descent,
to crash and burn
in life's torment.

JUST ANOTHER WORD

A patch of green
    on desert sand—
    made me think
    about us,
    how we came together,
    our arms spanning an ocean,
    reaching out,
    never giving up—
    even when hope
    seemed like a distant concept,
    just another word.

I MISS YOU

My pen knows no limit when it comes to expressing my love for you, but when we're apart, I miss you beyond words.

Tokoriki

Here it is—
    my island,
    the sweet scent
    of frangipani,
    carried in the arms
    of a gentle breeze,
    serenaded by a sea—
    beating a slow rhythm
    on a golden drum.

How beautiful the moon—
    rising in balmy skies,
    where stars tumble
    into luminescent waves
    breaking on a distant reef.

Your body bathing
    in its light,
    skin the color
    of silver,
    reading Murakami
    by candlelight.

Memories—
    like a siren's song,
    calling me back
    to this place,
    where lovers
    come home.

A New Beginning

I read this morning that NASA had discovered a new planet capable of life. Somewhere faraway in another galaxy. A tiny blue dot found by a giant telescope. *"A New Beginning,"* the headline screamed.

Of course, all the enthusiastic words conveniently sidestepped the inconvenient truth. The reality of the hundred or so years it would take to reach this potential new home with our current technology. Which got me thinking, imagine if we could just click our fingers and magically travel there in an instant. Depart this dying planet we call Earth and start living in some new paradise. Would we?

A question I neatly folded into the back of my mind and took with me to lunch. Sitting in the pretty courtyard of my favorite restaurant, La Luna, which served the most wonderful Italian cuisine. The wine list alone was incentive enough to visit. A collection of rare and dusty bottles gifted to the place by a wealthy Italian countess in her will. The entire contents from her expansive cellar, which sat beneath a medieval castle. Just one of the many homes she owned back in the '80s.

Sophia lit a cigarette, a habit she had still failed to break throughout countless New Year's resolutions. Blowing the smoke upward into the warm afternoon air.

She was wearing a white flowing dress that accentuated her summer tan and flame-red hair. A pair of Karen Walker sunglasses framing her pretty face and pink lipsticked lips.

"So pleased you managed to get a table outside and one with plenty of shade," she said smiling.

It was, in my humble opinion, one of the better tables in the courtyard. Tucked neatly away in the far corner, underneath a crooked olive tree whose branches reached over the ivy-clad brick wall. A perfect spot for lovers to chink glasses with starry eyes, or spies to trade dark secrets, or in our case, two close friends who loved to talk about all manner of nonsense.

"Well, I thought we were long overdue a decent lunch," I replied, eyeing the pack of Jolly Rogers lying next to her Hermès purse with envy. I took out a shiny new silver contraption from my light blue linen jacket and quickly took in two deep lungfuls of clove vape juice.

"Finished your book last night," Sophia said, grinning. "Loved it. I think it's the best you've written. More reflective, much deeper, and I'm relieved you resisted to jump on the poetry bandwagon and fill it with just six-word, incomprehensible sweet nothings and lazy metaphors."

I had recently received an advanced copy of my new book, *Cult of Two*, from the publisher, and as always, I had given it to Sophia to read for her no-holds-barred opinion.

"Oh, I think I'm just as guilty of writing the odd one-liner. So much can often be said with so little," I replied, taking another hit of vape and laughing.

"Yes, but you know what I mean. A lot of what's written today and called *poetry* is little more than senseless fluff, meaningless drivel."

"That's a bit harsh. Some of it is pretty damn good and it's wildly popular with a lot of people."

Sophia laughed. "Yes, I guess you're right. I am guilty of sometimes *hate reading* books."

"Well, since you're wearing your bitchy hat, what do you honestly think about my latest book?"

"I told you. I loved it. The poetry seems a lot more introspective, real, and the prose is beautifully melancholic and thought provoking. It reads like you've gone up a level. Lifted your game. You really should stop dithering and write a fucking novel."

The waiter politely interrupted us, pencil poised, and ran through the specials of the day.

I chose the platter of calamari to share and the smoked salmon linguini. Sophia removed her sunglasses, scanned the menu quickly and selected the slow-braised lamb shoulder served with roasted seasonal vegetables. A stunning bottle of Pietracupa Greco di Tufo on the side.

Our glasses were quietly topped up with sparkling water and the waiter slipped away, moving in between the crowded tables like a champion ballroom dancer.

Sophia took a sip of water and lit another cigarette. I couldn't resist it any longer. I reached across the table and I took one from the pack.

"Here you go," she chuckled gleefully, flicking her gold lighter with expert dexterity, its flame mocking my lack of willpower.

No matter how much I had tried to convince myself otherwise, no amount of sickly sweet vape juice and plumes of fake smoke could come close to the real thing.

Old habits die hard.

—

As usual, the food was amazing. I watched with some regret as our waiter took away our empty dessert plates, leaving behind just our wine glasses, the bottle of wine, and a clean ashtray.

Sophia leaned back in her chair and sighed.

"If only we could eat like this all the time. I mean, imagine being able to afford having your own personal chef to whip up delicious treats whenever you felt like it. Now, that would be like living in a perfect world."

I reached for another cigarette from Sophia's pack, lit it, and blew a smoke ring.

"Speaking of perfect worlds, I read an interesting article this morning. Apparently NASA has discovered a new planet capable of life."

"Really? Well, what are we waiting for, let's go!" Sophia said, laughing.

I topped up our wine glasses and fired off the question that had been spinning around in my head all day.

"At the moment, it would take decades to travel to it, but what if you could just click your fingers and be there? Would you go? I mean on the basis that this new planet was already set up for living, just like Earth but without all the pollution, wars, and other miserable stuff. A new beginning."

Sophia drained the wine from her glass and gave me one of her infamous intense stares. "And where's the inevitable *'but?'* You're selling the dream and it sounds a little too good to be true."

"Okay, here's the *but*. It's a one-way trip. No going back. You have to leave all your family and friends behind. A brand new start."

"Ha! I can already see a plot hole in your question," she replied. "Why couldn't they just click their fingers too and come with me?"

"Yes, yes, I know. Fair point. I guess this hypothetical question is more about the choice of living in a possible utopia versus remaining in a morally bankrupt world."

"It's a ridiculous question and a loaded one. I would obviously choose to stay given that choice. I couldn't bear the thought of leaving my family and friends behind no matter how marvelous this new planet was or could be."

I stubbed my cigarette out and poured another wine. Sophia's answer sparked another thought.

"Makes me think of how terrible it must be for refugees. How they often have no choice but to flee their homes and seek refuge overseas in some new country that is totally alien to them. Far away from family and friends. Everything they have ever known."

"I think we can never truly know just how traumatic that must be. Even if it is to a safer place than the one they have been forced to leave behind," Sophia said, the sadness clearly visible on her face.

"I agree. It's incomprehensible. Unless you have walked in their shoes you honestly have no idea."

"Puts our petty problems into perspective," Sophia said, reaching for my hand across the table. "We are so blessed to live the lives we do."

Sophia was dead right.

———

It was a stunning sunset. A giant melting sun gripping hold of puffy tropical clouds before letting go and collapsing into a calm sea.

A refreshing, cool breeze blew through the open window of Sophia's bedroom—the scent of salt and seaweed in the air.

I always felt at peace here. In the little beach house that overlooked the half-moon shaped bay. A private sanctuary hidden away high on a hill, where palm trees and whistling birds completed the pretty picture.

"A penny for your thoughts," Sophia said.

"I love this place," I replied, turning away from the window to meet her dreamy gaze. "Almost as much as I love you."

She was sitting up in the bed, a white sheet wrapped around her, covering her nakedness.

"Oh, stop it. Don't start getting all sentimental. Where is my cynical poet? My Mr. Misery?"

"I wouldn't call myself cynical, just perhaps a realist. And as for being a misery, I consider myself an optimist actually."

My response made Sophia burst out laughing. "Ha! Who are you trying to convince? Not so long ago you were entertaining the idea of packing your bags and heading off to that new planet."

I felt a witty reply building inside my head but before I could deliver it, Sophia beckoned me back to the bed with her finger.

"Let's continue this conversation in bed," she said grinning. "My legs can't wait to hear what your hands have to say."

—

It was past midnight.

We sat on yellow-striped deck chairs in Sophia's garden staring at the full moon. Taking swigs from a bottle of rum. The perfume of sex clinging to our warm skin. It seemed like our friendship had set sail on a different course. One that didn't need a map or compass to find paradise.

Sophia handed me my book, opened to a page marked by a folded corner.

"It's one thing to read a book but quite another to hear the voice behind the words speak them," she said, lighting a cigarette and blowing the smoke into the night air. "Read to me, my love, and please never stop."

—

Beneath the Desert Stars

I found myself
beneath the desert stars,
far away—
from a world
where love existed,
lost in conversation
with a silent
constellation,
wishing you
were mine.

Why is it so—
when hands let go,
it is the heart
that holds on tight,
like the final flicker
of a fading star—
taken by the light.

WISDOM

Wisdom—
    it is said,
    comes with the passing of years,
    but it seems nothing
    is really learned,
    between the lines dug
    on a furrowed brow,
    the repeated mistakes
    neatly buried,
    by my own hand—
    while yours continues
    to push the plough.

LIVE YOUR LIFE

Don't live your life based on other people's expectations. Listen to the person who knows you best. You.

RESPECT

So she gave
    you a smile,
    but that's no excuse,
    to justify
    your unwanted
    attention.

It's just an illusion,
    your fucked-up delusion,
    not a permission
    to take her to bed.

It's time
    to respect,
    instead of expect,
    to acknowledge
    the wrongs
    of the past.

And when she
    says *no,*
    you know it
    means no,
    and just once
    it needs only
    be said.

I WAS WRONG

For years I convinced myself that my actions were driven by sound judgment and unwavering confidence. I was wrong. It was my stupid ego that led me down this lonely road to nowhere.

TAKE NOT

Take not what is mine
    to never give,
    for this heart
    is a ring
    on another's finger,
    just leave me be,
    free my thoughts
    from this temptation,
    hear my cry
    for quiet mercy,
    please—
    just one more kiss
    before you go.

FRIDAY EPIPHANY

It is rare to find an unhappy fool but all too easy to spot a miserable genius.

TRUTH OR DARE?

Truth or dare? How we loved to play that party game as teenagers. No matter which one we chose, it was just all a bit of fun. No serious repercussions. Except perhaps that time when Mark jumped off the shed roof and spent the rest of the summer break with his leg in plaster. Even when Penny admitted she had a crush on her sports teacher, Miss Waddle, *I think that was her name*, we all just shrugged it off with howls of laughter.

Whatever happened to those innocent times?

When did it all change?

How did we end up here?

Straitlaced and judgmental. Boring adults who bite their lips before speaking. Too afraid to say what we really think and feel. Tiptoeing our way through inane dinner conversations. Playing a brand new game. Where telling the truth has become the ultimate dare.

A LOVE THIS STRONG

When the last drop of youth has been sipped, and we become like autumn leaves, waiting patiently for that final gust of wind to blow—the love we share will only grow stronger.

THE BIRTHDAY PARTY

A frosty white
    paints morning grass,
    the crunch of footsteps
    startling crows,
    a black cloud rising
    in misty gray,
    a veil worn thin
    by winter sun,
    a fallen love
    marked by a marble cross,
    white roses placed
    on scattered leaves,
    from trees laid bare
    by death's release,
    another year—
    no candles burn,
    no cake is cut,
    no wishes blown,
    our happiness tied
    with ribbons red,
    the gift you gave
    once made for two,
    I now give back
    to you—
    alone.

IT'S MY LIFE

Who are you to tell me what to do and how to live?

Stop thinking your mistakes are mine to own. Take back the cracked mirror you so arrogantly hold up to my face and remember who broke it in the first place.

Leave me the fuck alone to build my paper castles.

Or burn them to the ground.

CAROUSEL

The relationship was going nowhere but that's what I loved about it. Uncomplicated and predictable. Like riding on a beautiful carousel with a pocketful of coins.

YOUR VOICE

How I longed to hear your voice again, my hand beneath the sheets, eyes slowly closing—listening to every single word. It wasn't just what you said, *but how you said it*, that kept me up at night.

A DREAM

A row of doors
    in a haunted hallway,
    red, black, orange,
    and blue,
    one handle warm—
    a faint trace of you
    lingering still.

I open it—
    walking into a room
    filled with photographs,
    pinned to peeling
    wallpaper walls,
    every one a memory—
    a reminder of you.

Do you remember
    how we laughed—
    smoking a joint
    on the Ferris wheel,
    the moonlight
    framing your face,
    how we kissed
    at the top,
    the heady taste
    of ash and sex,
    spilling from lips
    that cried for more—
    now deathly quiet
    in the morning light.

STRIPTEASE

Your clothes fall—
 like white petals torn
 one by one,
 slowly,
 a tease performed
 with clever fingers,
 until nothing is left
 but the reveal,
 my yellow daisy,
 standing naked—
 your piercing eyes
 undressing me,
 your turn,
 they whisper.

THE WEDDING PRESENT

The big day had finally arrived and it was chaos. Mandy was beside herself, rearranging the flowers for the fifth time, placing long stem white tulips into vases scattered around the bedroom. All the guests would be arriving any minute now and she hadn't even sorted the bottles of champagne and glasses. Rupert watched her race around the room in the reflection of the wardrobe mirror, a smile breaking across his cleanly shaved face, as his fingers wrestled with the white bowtie.

"Oh here, let me do that," said Simon as he waltzed into the room wearing a white tuxedo, looking like a million dollars. He quickly took control of Rupert's bowtie drama and tied it perfectly in less than ten seconds.

Rupert kissed him on the cheek. "What would I do without you? How do I look?"

Simon gave him a quick look up and down. Rupert was wearing a matching white tuxedo but with a scarlet handkerchief tucked into the top pocket of his jacket. "You are the best looking husband this side of the river."

"Not yet," Rupert replied grinning.

"And bloody never at this rate!" Mandy screamed. "Come on you two, sort yourselves out. We have a wedding to get done."

The doorbell rang.

Mandy started to panic again.

—

It was Rupert's idea to exchange vows in bed. He was a big John Lennon fan and wanted to channel John and Yoko's famous 1969 "bed-ins for peace" vibe. Simon loved the idea too but *only if it was just for one day and not a whole week,* he had repeatedly stressed to a bemused Rupert.

The ceremony had gone smoothly. Simon's sister, Mandy, presided over the exchange of vows. She was a part-time marriage celebrant and wedding planner. Even the Skype call from Simon and Mandy's parents had gone off without a hitch. Wishing the happy couple all the very best from the cabin of their cruise ship sailing in the Mediterranean. The wedding had been a spur of the moment decision, another of Rupert's bright ideas, so there was no way they could get back for it in time.

When the happy couple exchanged identical gold rings and kissed for the first time as husband and husband, the bedroom had erupted with cheers and loud applause. The love so powerful in the room, barely a dry eye could be seen on any of the guests.

And now that the official part was done and dusted, the party was in full swing.

Twelve of their dearest and closest friends knocked back the French champagne, cracked jokes, and chatted with the happy couple. Who were laying in their huge bed, propped up on pillows, a pile of neatly wrapped wedding presents sitting on a side table. ABBA's "I Do, I Do, I Do, I Do, I Do" blaring out of the Bose speakers.

Mandy topped up Simon's glass with more champagne and he caught the worried expression on her face. He knew what was wrong. Not everything had gone to plan. But before he could say anything, she quickly walked off, checking her watch repeatedly.

The doorbell rang.

"I'll get it!" Mandy shouted, running out of the bedroom in a flash.

—

Rupert was halfway through telling a particularly filthy joke when Mandy poked her head around the bedroom door and caught his eye with a wave of her hand. He stopped short of the punchline and called out to her.

"What is it, Darling?" he shouted over the music.

Mandy hit a button on a remote and the music stopped. Everyone turned in her direction.

"Rupert, you have a special delivery. It's in the living room," she said nervously.

"Well, well, well, what could it be?" Rupert replied excitedly, as he hopped out of bed. "You coming, husband, to have a peek?"

Simon gave Mandy a quick glance. She nodded back. "No, I'll wait here. You go. I'll keep the bed warm."

Rupert giggled and took Mandy by the hand. "Come on love, let's go see what all this fuss is about."

———

In an instant, the blood literally drained from Rupert's face. His smile wiped clean.

"What the fuck are you doing here?" he said angrily.

Mandy gently squeezed his hand. "Just listen to what he has to say."

Standing in the living room was a tall, elderly man dressed in a gray suit, yellow tie, and neatly polished black shoes. A white ribbon had been tied around his waist, complete with an oversized bow. He looked Rupert in the eyes and spoke. His voice already starting to break.

"Hi, Son. Sorry I'm late. Plane was delayed . . ."

Rupert cut him off. "Fuck your excuses. I don't care. Just get the fuck out of my house!"

The old man stood up straight, took a deep breath, and continued talking.

"Son, I will go. But not before I say something I should have said to you years ago. I'm so sorry. Sorry for how I've treated you in the past. Sorry for my ignorance. I'm ashamed. Deeply ashamed, for not accepting you for who you are. I was wrong to turn my back on you. When we lost your mother, my world collapsed, and when you told me you were gay, it felt like I had lost you too. It was all me, never you. It's my fault our relationship broke down. The blame rests with me and I wish I could turn back the clock. I honestly do. I'm not asking for your forgiveness and I don't want to spoil your big day. But when Simon tracked me down and rang me, when he told me you were getting married, my heart sank. Made me realize what a fool I've been. How much time we have lost because of me. I never stopped loving you, Son, and I wanted you to know that. Anyway, I'll leave you be now, get on my way."

Rupert said nothing and just watched silently as his dad tried to undo the white ribbon Mandy had wrapped around him. His arthritic fingers shaking as they tugged at the bow. Rupert could see the tears welling up in his father's tired eyes.

"Let me do that," said Mandy in a quiet voice.

"No. I'll do it." Rupert said as he walked over to his dad and hugged him. The old man bursting into tears, sobbing uncontrollably into his son's shoulder. Rupert patted his back. "Hush now. You'll ruin this bloody tux and it cost a fortune."

The old man looked up. A faint smile appearing on his wrinkled face. "Good to see you haven't lost your sense of humor, Son."

"Okay, enough of this," said Rupert, brushing away a tear from his eye. "You'll set me off crying too at this rate. And this is a wedding. Not a fucking funeral! Now come on, Dad, it's time you met my fabulous husband."

The old man took a comb from his pocket, and ran it through his thinning white hair. "I'd love to, Son,"

A QUICK KISS

A quick kiss,
    that's all it was—
    like a toe dipped in
    a swimming pool,
    to test the water
    before diving in,
    a licked finger
    held up to the air,
    trying to tell
    which direction
    the wind was blowing.

A quick kiss
    that's all it was—
    my arrow shot
    from shaky bow,
    just another miss.

MY GRANDMOTHER

You had already gone before you left this earth. Just a trace of you remained in those final days. A faint voice on the end of a phone, a sudden glimmer of recognition, only to be forgotten in the same breath. My heart breaking as I realized we would never speak again of *Dr. Who*—the sun quickly setting on all those apple pie days.

It's the happy memories I hang on to now. And when I squeeze my eyes shut, I can still see you smiling at me. Hair neatly done. Makeup applied with care. The twinkle in your eye when you laughed at one of my silly stories.

I know, deep down, that's exactly how you would want me to remember you.

The love we had, a bond so strong, that not even death could take it away.

Your passing from this world reminded me that we are all just dominos. Lined up in a neat little row on life's kitchen table. Waiting for our time to fall.

And when my turn comes, I know you will be there, ready to catch me.

A SUMMER GONE

No subtle hint
   of summer left,
   a season passes by—
   no fond farewell,
   a lover lost,
   a sea gone silent
   in its shell.

So a toast
   to fading sunlight,
   shots of coffee
   sipped at three,
   pour whiskey
   into paper cups,
   collect wood
   from broken trees—
   for what is left
   is nothing more,
   than whispers
   on the wind,
   for a summer came
   and quickly went—
   no trace of it
   remains.

IN THE BLINK OF AN EYE

How would I describe the end of our relationship?
A blowtorch held to a tiny cube of ice.

YOU CAME INTO MY LIFE

You came into my life
 like a swirling tornado,
 breaking everything
 you touched,
 my confidence
 left in ruins,
 my belief in love
 torn apart,
 and when the dust
 finally settled,
 all that remained
 was the debris
 of a heart,
 scattered across
 a lonely wasteland.

THE CULT OF TWO

It was lust that brought us together.

An overwhelming urge to fuck.

A raging fire burning out of control.

Consuming us both.

Our sex-filled fantasies played out in seedy motel rooms. Fueled by cheap liquor, party drugs, and wet panties.

No masters.

Just slaves bound by depravity and self-destruction.

Phones smashed.

Bridges burned.

Just you.

Just me.

In this dangerous cult of two.

BROKEN UMBRELLA

You said you would love me forever and always be there. But when the sky collapsed and came crashing down, all you left me with was a broken umbrella.

WELCOME HOME

Come to me quietly
    in this waking hour,
    the purple pause
    between darkness
    and muted light,
    the call of the magpie
    beckoning the dawn,
    crisp sheets cast aside
    by sleepy fingers,
    a rush of cold
    before the trickle
    of glowing warmth,
    legs sliding into
    a waiting bed,
    your naked body
    spooning into mine,
    the scent of toothpaste
    on your lips,
    a homecoming
    softly sealed,
    by a lover's
    morning kiss.

CROWN OF THORNS

The garland of roses
    you promised,
    nothing more
    than empty words
    spoken in jest,
    with me as the punch line—
    cruelly mislead,
    crying alone,
    a crown of thorns
    on my head.

MELTING ICE CREAM

"You seem restless tonight," I said, as we sat down for dessert.

"Oh, it's nothing really. It'll pass. Just pour me another glass of wine," she replied with a wry smile. "But if you're really concerned for my well-being—lift up my skirt, bend me over this table, and fuck me until the ice cream melts."

Always You

It feels like I have known you all my life and every life I have ever lived.

THE PASSING OF YEARS

We are too busy knocking back the martinis of youth—our life nothing more than a rushing blur reflected in a rain-streaked window. Time is a slow-moving train wreck we only begin to notice when it's all too late.

No More Wishes

I swim with sharks
    when darkness comes,
    the butter melting
    on a plate,
    my coffee cup
    untouched,
    chasing shadows
    inside my head,
    wishing I had
    more wishes left,
    to waste again
    on you.

A WITHERED HEART

Shut the fuck up—
   I'm tired of your
   empty promises,
   give those lying
   lips a break,
   save your breath
   for some other
   hopeless fool—
   go find another
   pretty distraction,
   to remove the pickles
   from your burger,
   while you feast
   on their naivety,
   never satisfied—
   until you wring
   the last drop of trust
   from their withered heart,
   like you did to me.

JUST YOU

I never asked for the moon, or a diamond ring, or some mansion high up on the hill. All I ever wanted was you—just you.

WINTER OF SUMMERS

I don't think either of us were searching for anyone. We were just two lost souls drawn together by circumstance. Travelers walking along the same stretch of lonely road, the well-trodden path to redemption. Looking for meaning in this meaningless life. Strangers who became more than just friends, over a bottle of vodka in a bar, sheltering from a blizzard.

The next morning we moved what little possessions we carried in our backpacks into a cabin by the frozen lake. Handing over a month's rent to the grizzled man wearing a rabbit fur hat. His eyebrow raised when we said we weren't married. Lighting a crumpled cigarette between his wrinkled lips as he pointed out the dusty furniture, dented fridge, little gas cooker, and fireplace. Walking us into the tiny bedroom and patting the bed with his giant hand, a small sneer creeping across his rugged face.

Rachel smiled awkwardly. I felt my cheeks blushing red. We hadn't crossed this line yet, where kisses became so much more.

"I'll leave you two to settle in. Don't forget to prime the water pump and keep the generator topped up in case the power goes," he said in a deep voice.

We nodded like anxious children in front of a scary headmaster, trying our best to hide the fact we honestly didn't have a clue. A wave of relief sweeping over us as the old man pulled the creaky front door closed behind him.

"Left or right side?" Rachel asked laughing. Her nervousness disguised with playful banter as she hopped onto the bed, making the decision for me.

—

The weeks passed slowly as we both slipped easily into the roles of make-believe lovers. I spent most days camped on the tatty brown sofa, head buried in a book, cooking in the evenings and only venturing away from the cabin to visit the general store in town. To withdraw cash from the ATM, pick up groceries, and buy bottles of wine. My savings account was well topped up by the sale of my apartment back in Vancouver. A place where my old life lay in ruins. Another time, a different story.

Rachel was far more industrious. Waking at dawn to write on her laptop, a collection of poetry she hoped to turn into a book one day. Her way of making sense of a broken marriage, she told me. A cathartic journey taken with fingers that had spent too much time wiping away tears from her soft gray eyes. When she wasn't writing, and the sun was shining, she would be outside building snowmen. Using carrots to give them erect cocks. Laughing at my frequent eye rolls whenever I discovered a new one.

The nights we spent playing cards with an old deck we had found in a wooden chest of drawers, along with a large collection of '70s porn magazines. Not that we needed any encouragement to fuck. It became one of our regular evening activities. So much so, it caused our old bed to break, a leg suddenly snapping, sending us rolling off the mattress onto the floor. After the initial shock of landing on our bare asses, all we could do was giggle. Rachel, always the resourceful one, managed to prop up the bed with a log found in the firewood pile. After that mini-disaster, we kept the bed solely for sleeping. Choosing instead to have sex everywhere else in the cabin. We even did it outside one afternoon. Up against a tree that towered above the roof and threatened to come crashing down every time a fierce storm hit.

Yet for all the physical intimacy, we were still mysteries to each other. I had tried not to bore Rachel with the nitty gritty of my doomed relationship, and she was always reluctant to talk about her past. When I did once ask her about her husband, she quickly shut me down with a frosty glare and screamed, *"You don't need to know, just leave it at that!"* So I kept things simple, lighthearted, and wonderfully superficial.

—

One Friday morning I did the unforgivable. While Rachel was outside ice fishing on the lake, I took a quick peek through the pile of pages she had written. Nervously peering out of the frosty window every so often, just in case I would be caught in the act. I knew what I was doing was wrong, but curiosity got the better of my decency.

There was one particular piece that jumped out at me.

Revenge

Did you feel the blade?
cold metal slicing
through butter skin,
your blood—
the color of strawberry jam,
sticky upon my fingers.

The gurgling opera of death—
such sweet notes
played on a red stage,
soft murmurings
of a cheating heart,
slowly stilled to silence,
a throat cut,
eyes rolling backward.

To think I loved you once—
my dearest dead husband,
never to rest in peace,
and when you burn
in the fires of Hell,
think of me—
the girl whose life
you took first.

While I read the lines for a second time, little did I know just how quickly a dark serendipity would change everything in an instant.

The distant wailing of police sirens made my body jolt upright, the page falling out of my hands. My head spun back to the window. I could see the silhouette of Rachel getting out of her chair and standing up on the blanket of icy white.

I felt the hairs rise on the back of my neck. My heart sinking as I raced out the front door and ran toward the lake. A couple of police cars skidded to a halt near me. I heard the noise of an ice drill starting up.

As I got closer to Rachel, I could see what she was doing. Her arms vibrating as she frantically cut away at the hole in the ice, making it wider.

"Rachel!" I screamed, a large cloud of breath exploding from my lips.

Rachel dropped the drill and stared in my direction. A quiet smile breaking across her rosy cheeks. Behind me I could hear voices yelling. I turned around and saw the police coming, guns drawn, and a barking dog tugging at its leash, held by the old man who had rented us the place.

I looked back at Rachel, panic surging through me, only to be met again by that serene smile.

"I'll never forget you." Her words reaching me before I could wrap my arms around her.

In a matter of seconds she was gone. Not even a splash of water to mark her descent into the hole, as she plunged feet first under the lake.

To be lost forever.

—

How can I forget the warmth of your body, the love that burned brightly within our hearts? You were my winter of summers.

THANK YOU

As the curtain falls on *Winter of Summers* and my words slip away into the shadows, I bid you a fond farewell.

For me, it's the saddest part of writing a book.

I know many of you like to read my books more than once. Which gives me some small comfort. Knowing we will find each other once more, somewhere within these pages.

If the stars collide, and I get really lucky, perhaps we'll meet up again in one of my other books.

Dirty Pretty Things, Bitter Sweet Love, or even *Smoke & Mirrors*.

Until then, please don't be a stranger. Let's stay in touch on my official Facebook, Twitter, and Instagram pages. I'd love to know which poems, pieces of prose, or short stories resonated with you.

Thank you for your wonderful support.

It means everything to me.

Love always,

—Michael x

ACKNOWLEDGMENTS

A big thank you to my literary agent, Al Zuckerman, for everything you do for me. I had such a wonderful time with you and Claire in Sydney. I can't wait to catch up again in New York! Many thanks to Samantha Wekstein too, and all the team at Writers House, New York.

Thank you so much, Kirsty Melville, Patty Rice, and everyone at Andrews McMeel, for all your enthusiasm, hard work, and for bringing a *Winter of Summers* into the world. Kirsty, I will always remember that beautiful lunch we had at Balmoral Beach. I look forward to the next one and hope Patty will be there to help us finish another bottle of stunning wine.

Tinca Veerman, you have so many amazing artworks, choosing just one is an almost impossible task. This is our fourth book cover together and I love it. Thank you, as always.

To Oliver, my son who is now taller than me, (yes, I finally admit it), I love you so much. Not a day goes by without me thinking of you and just how proud I am to be your Dad.

Mum and Dad, nothing makes me happier than when we are all sitting around the one table. Thanks for making your last trip to New Zealand so memorable. Especially our lunch at Café Hanoi.

To my grandmother, Doris, who passed away this year, you will always live on in my heart and in this book.

To Genevieve, who is always there for me, thank you for being you. I had such a great time with you and Ryder in Auckland. Hurry up and come back.

Thank you to all my friends, you know who you are.

And to all my lovely readers, I can't thank you enough.

ABOUT THE AUTHOR

Michael Faudet is the author of the international bestsellers *Dirty Pretty Things*, *Bitter Sweet Love*, and *Smoke & Mirrors*. His books have been nominated in the Goodreads Choice Awards for Best Poetry. *Dirty Pretty Things* was also selected by Sylvia Whitman, the owner of the iconic Shakespeare and Company bookstore in Paris, as one of her personal favorite books of 2016.

He frequently explores the intricacies of love, loss, relationships, and sex in poetry, prose, and short stories. His lyrical and often sensual writing continues to attract readers from all around the world.

Before turning his hand to writing books, Michael enjoyed a successful career in advertising as an award-winning executive creative director. He managed creative departments and developed advertising campaigns for major brands in many countries.

Michael is represented by the literary agency Writers House, New York. He currently lives in New Zealand in a little house by the sea with girlfriend and author Lang Leav.

INDEX

Andrews McMeel Publishing
a division of Andrews McMeel Universal
1130 Walnut Street, Kansas City, Missouri 64106

www.andrewsmcmeel.com

www.michaelfaudet.com

18 19 20 21 22 BVG 10 9 8 7 6 5 4 3 2 1

ISBN: 978-1-4494-9639-5

Library of Congress Control Number: 2018954751

Cover art by Tinca Veerman
www.tincaveerman.com

Editor: Patty Rice
Designer, Art Director: Julie Barnes
Production Editor: David Shaw
Production Manager: Cliff Koehler

ATTENTION: SCHOOLS AND BUSINESSES
Andrews McMeel books are available at quantity discounts with bulk purchase for educational, business, or sales promotional use. For information, please e-mail the Andrews McMeel Publishing Special Sales Department: specialsales@amuniversal.com.

Join Michael Faudet on the following:

Facebook   **Twitter**   **Instagram**   **Tumblr**